So wird es gemacht:

Öffne das LÜK®-Lösungsgerät und lege die Plättchen in den bedruckten Deckel. Jetzt kannst du auf den Plättchen und auf dem Geräteboden die Zahlen 1 bis 24 sehen.

Beispiel: Seite 2
The Indefinite Article a/an

Nimm Plättchen 1 und lies Aufgabe 1:
This is a/an English book. Entscheide nun, welcher Artikel richtig ist. Hier ist es *an*. Daneben steht die 12. Das ist die Feldzahl, auf die du das Plättchen legst, also Plättchen 1 auf die Zahl 12 im Lösungsgerät. Die Zahl **1** soll nach oben zeigen.

So arbeitest du weiter, bis alle Plättchen im Geräteboden liegen. Schließe dann das Gerät und drehe es um. Öffne es von der Rückseite.

Wenn du das bei der Übungsreihe abgebildete Lösungsmuster siehst, hast du alle Aufgaben richtig gelöst.

Passen einige Plättchen nicht in das Muster, dann hast du dort Fehler gemacht. Drehe diese Plättchen da, wo sie liegen, um, schließe das Gerät, drehe es um, und öffne es wieder. Jetzt kannst du sehen, welche Aufgaben du falsch gelöst hast.
Nimm diese Plättchen heraus und suche die richtigen Ergebnisse. Kontrolliere dann noch einmal. Stimmt jetzt das Muster?

Das System ist für alle Übungen dasselbe: Die roten Aufgabennummern im Heft entsprechen immer den LÜK-Plättchen aus dem Lösungsgerät.
Die schwarzen Zahlen hinter den Lösungen sagen dir, auf welche Felder des Lösungsgerätes die Plättchen gelegt werden müssen.

Und nun viel Spaß!

The Indefinite Article *(unbestimmter Artikel)* a/an

Tip: use "a" before consonants
use "an" before vowels (a, e, i, o, u). } singular
This is a book. He is an old man.

(Achtung: "a/an" steht nie vor Nomen im Plural!)

1	This is a • 4 an • 12 English book.
2	He has a • 15 an • 20 car.
3	John is an • 14 a • 7 good taxi driver.
4	The man is a • 11 an • 17 professor.
5	She is an • 2 a • 13 old grandmother.
6	He is drinking a • 16 an • 14 cup of coffee.
7	They have a • 3 an • 18 lovely house.
8	It is a • 19 an • 6 American hamburger.
9	She is wearing an • 10 a • 8 green jacket.
10	Look! There's an • 18 a • 1 bird in the garden.
11	He is eating an • 13 a • 5 piece of chocolate.
12	Give me a • 4 an • 22 pound of sugar.
13	The mouse has got an • 19 a • 24 piece of cheese.
14	My father has got a • 2 an • 21 old cupboard.
15	I have got a • 24 an • 20 idea.
16	This is a • 3 an • 23 expensive pen.
17	You must get on a • 9 an • 14 number 3 bus.
18	The cowboy is drinking an • 23 a • 19 glass of milk.
19	The girl is wearing an • 10 a • 13 old ring.
20	He is driving an • 18 a • 16 old taxi.
21	A • 20 An • 14 airport has got many planes.
22	The house has got an • 7 a • 22 red door.
23	An • 17 A • 3 egg is white or brown.
24	There is an • 13 a • 12 animal in our garden.

2

Singular (one) and Plural Nouns (more than one)

Tip: Noun + "s" = plural form of nouns:

One lamp (singular) ➜ two lamps (plural),
a book ➜ books.

Find the correct answer – singular or plural?

1. Kevin has got two   pencil • 2   pencils • 19 .

2. They are playing with a   hamsters • 16   hamster • 21 .

3. The hamster is on my   beds • 1   bed • 24 .

4. Vera has got three   apples • 20   apple • 18 .

5. There are five   number • 12   numbers • 17   on the blackboard.

6. Three   boy • 5   boys • 22   are playing table-tennis.

7. We have got a new   computers • 13   computer • 15 .

8. Ronald is cooking a   hamburger • 13   hamburgers • 14 .

9. She has two very nice   rooms • 23   room • 10 .

10. It is a yellow   taxis • 7   taxi • 18 .

11. Jim has got six   CD players • 14   CD player • 8 .

12. The teacher has only got one   book • 16   books • 19 .

13. My sister is writing a   letter • 7   letters • 17 .

14. I have three   sister • 16   sisters • 9 .

15. There is one   clocks • 4   clock • 11   on the wall.

16. Dad has got two   cameras • 8   camera • 5 .

17. I have got three   cousins • 3   cousin • 18 .

18. Four   cup • 11   cups • 12   are on the kitchen table.

19. There are seven   bird • 16   birds • 4   in the cage.*

20. They are on their   bike • 6   bikes • 1 .

21. She is carrying two   handbags • 5   handbag • 9 .

22. That is my   chairs • 17   chair • 10 .

23. How many   brother • 13   brothers • 2   have you got?

24. I have got one   brother • 6   brothers • 16 .   * = Käfig

3

First, Second, Third Person Singular and Plural

		Singular	Plural
Tip: First Person = (1st)	→	I	we
Second Person = (2nd)	→	you	you
Third Person = (3rd)	→	he, she, it	they

1 She is sleeping in her bedroom.

3rd person singular | 10   1st person plural | 17

2 I have a very nice neighbour.

1st person singular | 1   1st person plural | 20

3 It is a big white house.

3rd person singular | 6   2nd person person singular | 11

4 He is on his black bike.

1st person plural | 3   3rd person singular | 9

5 They have lots of chocolate cake.

3rd person plural | 17   2nd person singular | 21

6 We must go to the post office.

3rd person singular | 8   1st person plural | 2

7 I am very happy today.

1st person plural | 24   1st person singular | 13

8 He has got a dirty pair of blue jeans.

1st person plural | 15   3rd person singular | 4

9 You have a lot of time to answer this.

2nd person singular | 5   1st person plural | 24

10 You all are my favourite pupils.

1st person singular | 6   2nd person plural | 18

11 She has a silly brother.

3rd person singular | 3   2nd person singular | 5

12 **They** are at a very nice hotel.
1st person plural | 17   3rd person plural | 14

13 **It** is still in your room.
1st person singular | 6   3rd person singular | 22

14 **I** always have orange juice for breakfast.
1st person singular | 7   1st person plural | 1

15 **You** have two minutes to clean your room!
2nd person singular | 11   3rd person plural | 22

16 **You** are the best boys and girls of all.
1st person plural | 14   2nd person plural | 21

17 **He** has his bike in the garage.
3rd person singular | 19   3rd person plural | 23

18 **It** is a lovely electric guitar.
3rd person plural | 8   3rd person singular | 12

19 **We** have an old tree in our garden.
2nd person plural | 3   1st person plural | 20

20 Have **you** got a TV in your room?
1st person plural | 17   2nd person singular | 16

21 Is **he** a good boy?
1st person singular | 15   3rd person singular | 23

22 Has **it** got enough petrol in its tank?
1st person singular | 20   3rd person singular | 8

23 Have **they** got enough money?
3rd person plural | 15   3rd person singular | 2

24 Is **she** in her seat?
2nd person singular | 10   3rd person singular | 24

Kevin and Caveman in the Classroom

Tip: Use "he/she" with people and "it" with things or animals in the 3rd person singular.

Replace (ersetze) the noun with a personal pronoun!

1 Caveman and Kevin are in the classroom.

| He | 6 | You | 20 | They | 7 |

2 The lamp is on.

| He | 17 | She | 3 | It | 9 |

3 Look! The blackboard is green.

| It | 12 | He | 1 | I | 24 |

4 The chairs are brown.

| We | 12 | You | 18 | They | 8 |

5 Caveman is eating the chalk.

| She | 21 | He | 5 | I | 11 |

6 The maps are on the bookshelf.

| He | 22 | It | 13 | They | 10 |

7 The map is on the desk.

| It | 3 | They | 12 | He | 19 |

8 Daniel has got a new school-bag.

| She | 3 | I | 2 | He | 1 |

9 Diana has got pretty hair.

| She | 11 | You | 4 | I | 17 |

10 Kevin is sitting in front of Caveman.

| She | 10 | We | 13 | He | 6 |

11 The ruler is very long.

| He | 4 | It | 2 | She | 8 |

12 My teacher and I sometimes have a lot of fun.

| He | 20 | They | 19 | We | 4 |

13 <u>This</u> is number thirteen.

It	19	I	6	We	12

14 <u>The flowers</u> are in our classroom.

It	5	She	14	They	21

15 <u>Kevin's book</u> is at home.

We	2	They	1	It	23

16 <u>Kevin's hat</u> is on Caveman's head.

It	20	He	21	You	7

17 <u>My mother and I</u> have breakfast together.

She	3	We	15	They	2

18 <u>Kevin and Caveman</u> have breakfast together, too.

He	9	We	16	They	24

19 <u>Marion</u> has got long hair.

It	14	She	16	They	2

20 <u>Marion and Suzanne</u> have got brown hair.

They	13	She	3	It	24

21 Is <u>the CD player</u> loud enough?

she	2	he	6	it	17

22 Have <u>Tim and Martin</u> got racing bikes?

we	4	they	22	it	20

23 Is <u>the dog</u> under the teacher's desk?

it	14	you	8	they	11

24 <u>Kevin</u> has got chewing-gum in the classroom.

She	2	He	18	We	12

Personal Pronoun (Subject Case)

Find the correct personal pronoun!

1 _____ am in the yellow bus.

He • 2   We • 13   I • 12

2 _____ are at the football match.

I • 6   It • 20   We • 9

3 _____ are ten and eleven years old.

He • 12   She • 20   They • 7

4 _____ is in my mother's cupboard.

It • 11   They • 16   You • 2

5 _____ am a good football-player, too.

He • 17   I • 1   It • 2

6 _____ is a nice girl.

They • 24   She • 10   You • 15

7 _____ is afraid of a mouse.

He • 21   We • 23   They • 16

8 _____ is a wonderful film.

They • 18   I • 20   It • 5

9 _____ are standing on my foot!

You • 8   I • 7   She • 11

10   is off to school.

He • 2   I • 10   They • 22

11   am hungry and thirsty.

He • 21   They • 10   I • 6

12   is very hot today.

It • 22   We • 3   They • 13

13   is fun to go skiing.

We • 19   I • 9   It • 23

14   are in the cafeteria.

He • 18   She • 12   We • 3

15   is too fat to play tennis.

I • 4   They • 12   He • 19

16 Is   in front of the school?

I • 15   she • 24   they • 4

17   is in the red box?

They • 7   It • 15   You • 23

18 Are   a good swimmer?

I • 1   he • 3   you • 20

19   aren't in the departement store.

They • 16   I • 9   It • 22

20   are the best reader in the class.

He • 5   I • 15   You • 18

21   is eight o'clock in the morning.

We • 23   You • 3   It • 14

22   am very happy this morning.

He • 6   You • 24   I • 4

23   is a very small orange.

We • 1   It • 17   They • 20

24   are in the building.

I • 8   They • 13   He • 19

The Pronoun (Object Case)

Tip: *Mir oder mich/dir oder dich?*
Ob Dativ (Wemfall) oder Akkusativ (Wenfall),
im Objektfall bleiben die Personalpronomen gleich.

	Singular	Plura
1. Person	me	us
2. Person	you	you
3. Person	him, her, it	then

Can you give <u>me</u> *(mir)* the book? It's the best book for <u>me</u> *(mich)*.

1 The customer is talking to *[the woman]*.

| him | 10 | her | 4 | us | 16 |

2 My neighbour always gives *[my brother and me]* something.

| we | 2 | them | 14 | us | 13 |

3 The mouse is in *[the cheese]* again.

| it | 18 | he | 16 | him | 21 |

4 She looks like *[the girl over there]*.

| me | 1 | she | 13 | her | 3 |

5 Martha always feeds *[the animals]* on Sunday.

| they | 2 | them | 23 | you | 18 |

6 Our maths teacher always gives **?** homework.

| it | 4 | us | 14 | they | 15 |

7 That is my bike over there, it belongs to **?** .

| me | 19 | he | 10 | they | 3 |

8 I have a piece of cake for *[Caveman]*.

| he | 24 | her | 19 | him | 10 |

9 Aunt Mary usually gives **?** a spoon on my birthday.

| it | 15 | me | 17 | you | 21 |

10 Peter washes *[the dinosaur]* at the car wash.

| it | 24 | her | 5 | them | 18 |

11 You must open *[the window]*.

| him | 14 | you | 22 | it | 9 |

12 Can you open *[the windows]*, please?

| it | 21 | you | 7 | them | 20 |

13 The policeman is shouting at *[Charlie]*.

| it | 5 | he | 14 | him | 16 |

14 Santa Claus is taking *[the toys]* out of his sack.

| them | 1 | her | 2 | him | 3 |

15 Show **?** your maths test.

| you | 11 | my | 4 | me | 5 |

16 The teacher can't help **?** with my homework.

| him | 23 | me | 15 | her | 13 |

17 The ice-cream man is talking to *[Sally]* now.

| she | 6 | us | 10 | her | 7 |

18 We love to see animals, so our teacher takes **?** to the zoo.

| him | 21 | her | 14 | us | 6 |

19 I like you. The flowers are for **?** .

| you | 8 | they | 19 | she | 2 |

20 The mouse is putting its head through *[the window]*.

| him | 23 | her | 9 | it | 22 |

21 The men are carrying *[the boxes]* into the van.

| it | 16 | them | 11 | us | 3 |

22 That is my pencil. Give it to **?** !

| me | 2 | us | 15 | you | 17 |

23 Don't ask me, ask *[Mr. Wright]*!

| us | 4 | he | 6 | him | 21 |

24 The boys and girls have got *[the answer]*.

| it | 12 | them | 14 | him | 3 |

Possessive Adjectives:
My, Your, His, Her, Its, Our, Your, Their

Besitzanzeigende Personalpronomen zeigen uns, zu wem jemand oder etwas gehört: Look! The cat is lying in <u>my bed</u>.

Find the correct pronoun!

1 You have **?** name and I have my name.

| me | 19 | you | 4 | your | 13 |

2 I like **?** mum's cooking best of all.

| its | 3 | my | 5 | me | 19 |

3 We visit **?** grandmother every weekend.

| she | 14 | us | 2 | our | 16 |

4 They are nice neighbours and **?** dog is nice, too.

| their | 2 | our | 4 | your | 18 |

5 I like Kevin and **?** friend, too.

| her | 7 | his | 21 | its | 16 |

6 You are reading **?** book now.

| your | 18 | they | 13 | me | 2 |

7 Michael and **?** dog go everywhere together.

| its | 6 | you | 16 | his | 11 |

8 Diana is dancing with **?** friend Marty.

| its | 17 | we | 23 | her | 19 |

9 The dog has got a bone in **?** mouth.

| its | 15 | my | 1 | your | 20 |

10 My sister and I go swimming in **?** swimming pool.

| we | 16 | our | 22 | they | 24 |

11 Have you got **?** ticket with you?

| me | 6 | your | 8 | its | 3 |

12 Caveman can't find **?** pet dinosaur.

| your | 5 | its | 17 | his | 24 |

13 Is your mum's cake good? Yes, **?** cake is very good.

| my | 12 | his | 14 | her | 1 |

14 We love to go camping and **?** camp is beautiful.

| us | 4 | our | 17 | they | 7 |

15 They can't find **?** rucksacks.

| we | 14 | their | 3 | you | 20 |

16 A kangaroo has **?** own pocket.

| my | 3 | its | 14 | you | 23 |

17 Look! The budgie is flying out of **?** cage.

| its | 23 | their | 15 | he | 1 |

18 Where is the manager? He is working at **?** desk.

| me | 9 | his | 4 | he | 11 |

19 Tell me about you and **?** family.

| its | 16 | my | 8 | your | 12 |

20 Take out your books and **?** homework.

| his | 2 | her | 15 | your | 7 |

21 They are listening to **?** radio.

| he | 6 | we | 23 | their | 9 |

22 I've got my book. Have you got **?** book, too?

| their | 17 | his | 3 | your | 6 |

23 Peter and Pat always wear **?** yellow pullovers.

| their | 20 | its | 21 | they | 10 |

24 Look! Christine isn't wearing **?** jeans.

| she | 4 | her | 10 | our | 16 |

Have/Have got
(have got = *im Sinne von „besitzen")*

Tip: "has" = 3rd person singular. He has a red book.
You have got a nice bike.

| 1 | I | has \| 10 **?** have \| 19 | got a fast skate-board. |

1 | I has \| 10 **?** have \| 19 got a fast skate-board.

2 | The girls have \| 21 **?** has \| 6 long hair.

3 | We has \| 16 **?** have \| 24 got an apple tree.

4 | Has \| 1 **?** Have \| 8 you got a garden?

5 | Robert has \| 5 **?** have \| 24 a lot of friends.

6 | Sandra haven't \| 4 **?** hasn't \| 22 got a skate-board.

7 | She hasn't \| 15 **?** haven't \| 7 got much money.

8 | Peter have \| 19 **?** has \| 13 got an orange basketball.

9 | Wendy has \| 11 **?** have \| 20 a very nice aunt.

10 | My father have \| 16 **?** has \| 18 got an alarm clock.

11 | Has \| 2 **?** Have \| 16 William got the right answer?

12 | Have \| 16 **?** Has \| 23 you got the right answer?

13 | Mike and Tom have \| 7 **?** has \| 12 many animals.

14 | They has \| 19 **?** have \| 9 some fish, too.

15 | What has \| 4 **?** have \| 23 you got in your school-bag?

16 | I have \| 20 **?** has \| 11 got a rubber mouse in my school-bag?

17 | The boy has \| 3 **?** have \| 15 got milk for the cat.

18 | Melanie and Monika have \| 12 **?** has \| 4 got pretty eyes.

19 | My pets have \| 4 **?** has \| 20 got a dirty cage.

20 | Your pet budgie have \| 14 **?** has \| 1 got a clean cage.

21 | I have \| 17 **?** has \| 3 my English lessons at half past nine.

22 | What has \| 6 **?** have \| 10 you got in your pocket?

23 | I has \| 10 **?** have \| 14 got a green frog* in my pocket.

24 | Ed has \| 6 **?** have \| 17 a pet frog, too.

* = *Frosch*

Professor Klinkenpot's Landing

Put the correct form of "to be" into the simple present tense. (Präsens)!

#	Options	Sentence
1	am 3 | is 12 | are 10	Professor Klinkenpot **?** on the dog house.
2	am 2 | is 16 | are 8	The dog and the cat **?** in the time-machine.
3	am 1 | is 9 | are 22	The woman **?** behind a tree.
4	am 20 | is 11 | are 10	Caveman **?** next to me.
5	am 4 | is 15 | are 7	I **?** Kevin.
6	am 4 | is 24 | are 7	Caveman and I **?** friends.
7	am 3 | is 2 | are 16	It **?** time for dinner.
8	am 23 | is 6 | are 4	My name **?** Kevin.
9	am 21 | is 16 | are 10	My dog and cat **?** friends, too.
10	am 1 | is 5 | are 3	They **?** very nice animals.
11	am 11 | is 5 | are 13	Dog food **?** good for cats, too.
12	am 18 | is 15 | are 1	The professor and Caveman **?** in the garden.
13	am 20 | is 24 | are 19	He **?** a professor.
14	am 9 | is 16 | are 20	They **?** hungry animals.
15	am 6 | is 22 | are 24	The woman **?** in the garden.
16	am 20 | is 23 | are 9	Caveman **?** funny and nice.
17	am 14 | is 15 | are 23	I **?** twelve years old.
18	am 6 | is 3 | are 21	We **?** always together.
19	am 13 | is 4 | are 20	I **?** very hungry.
20	am 18 | is 5 | are 22	I **?** Caveman's best friend.
21	am 3 | is 21 | are 16	Kevin and Caveman **?** having a lot of fun.
22	am 13 | is 7 | are 19	They **?** next to the machine.
23	am 2 | is 17 | are 16	It **?** full of dog food.
24	am 5 | is 14 | are 15	They **?** in the middle of it.

The Present Progressive

Tip: The present progressive (-ing form) is formed with the auxiliary verb
"to be" (am/is/are + verb + ing): He is drinking cola.
We use the progressive form when something is happening <u>now</u>
(wenn etwas <u>gerade</u> passiert und noch nicht zu Ende ist).

Put the sentences into the present progressive!

		am	is	are
1	The waiter _____ bringing the ice-cream.	11	7	23
2	The boy _____ pulling the girl's hair.	10	9	18
3	I _____ writing a letter to my Uncle Bill.	12	8	1
4	Look! The man _____ parking his car.	13	20	4
5	Martin and Sally _____ cleaning their rooms.	14	8	17
6	We _____ taking my brother to see Santa Claus.	11	22	10
7	The hamster _____ eating my socks.	24	4	2

	am	is	are	
8	5	20	1	Jill's cats _____ playing in mum's room.
9	23	14	9	I _____ flying Professor Klinkenpot's machine.
10	3	19	6	_____ you looking at the gorilla?
11	14	5	12	I _____ looking at my silly monkey.
12	6	19	3	They _____ cleaning his cage now.
13	2	21	19	We _____ eating the fish and chips.
14	4	22	12	The bell _____ ringing now.
15	9	24	11	My father and brother _____ shouting at me.
16	18	8	5	The milkman _____ bringing the milk.
17	10	16	15	Look! They _____ climbing onto the table.
18	2	24	8	The disc-jockey _____ playing my favourite song.
19	18	16	13	Everybody _____ singing the new song.
20	2	5	13	_____ you listening to the music?
21	10	5	7	Caveman _____ feeding his pet dinosaur.
22	9	21	15	Help! It _____ biting my left foot.
23	2	19	4	I _____ standing on my right foot.
24	19	10	18	The doctors _____ looking at my foot.

What Are They Doing at the Beach?

Find the correct picture!

1. Kevin and Caveman are getting into a boat.
2. A bird is sitting on a volleyball net.
3. The mouse is running across the volleyball net.
4. The girls are playing football.
5. Michael is paddling the canoe with his guitar.
6. We are watching TV on the beach.
7. Fat Freddy is eating spaghetti.
8. The girl in the bikini is lying in the sun.
9. The boys and girls are playing volleyball on the beach.
10. Curt is throwing cold water at the girl.
11. The big beachball is rolling into the water.
12. The baby is walking with an umbrella.
13. Mrs. Brown is putting suntan lotion on her legs.
14. They are singing around the campfire.
15. The ice-cream man is coming.
16. The dog is running after the cat.
17. Sandra is listening to pop music on her discman.
18. They are throwing the frisbee.
19. Mr. Shade is wearing dark sunglasses.
20. A man is drinking beer.
21. That man is reading a book in his chair.
22. The cat is swimming in the lake.
23. The man is selling hot dogs at the hot dog stand.
24. The girls are putting sand in a boy's hair.

19

6

24

12

15

14

22

7

3

16

4

10

1

17

13

8

11

21

20

18

23

2

5

9

Simple Present in the 3rd Person Singular → Verb + "s"

Tip: Caveman always burns his fingers on the hot potato.
He forgets the ending **"s"** with the verb in the <u>3rd Person Singular</u>.

Help Caveman!

1	Caveman	open • 3 opens • 14	the door for Kevin.
2	Mrs. Pratt	walk • 7 walks • 18	into the classroom.
3	The bell	rings • 21 ring • 17	at 8:00 o'clock every morning.
4	After the lesson the teacher	leave • 23 leaves • 13	the classroom, too.
5	She	wear • 2 wears • 9	a red pullover and blue jeans.
6	Willy never	listen • 14 listens • 17	to the teacher.
7	The headmaster sometimes	come • 24 comes • 5	into the room.
8	He	looks • 1 look • 13	for his pet dinosaur after school.
9	It usually	eats • 22 eat • 4	grass and yellow flowers.
10	Sometimes it even	drink • 12 drinks • 10	chocolate milk.
11	Ron never	shut • 19 shuts • 2	the window.
12	Vera	climbs • 6 climb • 10	onto the desk.

20

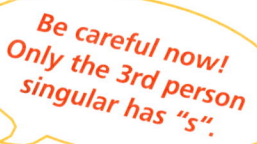

Be careful now! Only the 3rd person singular has "s".

13	The boys and girls	love • 19 loves • 5	speaking English.
14	Dinosaurs never	drinks • 6 drink • 23	beer.
15	Caveman and Kevin	play • 15 plays • 22	with a frisbee.
16	The other school	begins • 20 begin • 11	at 8:15.
17	Susan	cleans • 12 clean • 20	the blackboard on Tuesdays.
18	Curt and Kevin	clean • 16 cleans • 8	the blackboard on Wednesdays.
19	Kevin	buy • 9 buys • 11	Caveman a sandwich for lunch.
20	My friends	helps • 1 help • 8	Caveman with his English.
21	Ira	asks • 4 ask • 21	Caveman a question.
22	Kevin and his Mum	get • 24 gets • 18	a great idea.
23	Mrs. Pratt	write • 16 writes • 7	her name on the board.
24	The teachers	talk • 3 talks • 15	to them.

Spelling Rules for the 3rd Person Singular

Tip: Spelling Rules for 3rd Person Singular Present Tense after -ss, -sh, -ch *(Zischlaut)* = -es: wish ➜ Bob wishes; verbs ending with consonant + y = -ies: carry ➜ carries, verbs with a vowel + y = s: buy ➜ buys.
Exceptions *(Ausnahmen)*: go ➜ goes / do ➜ does.

		-s	-es	-ies
1	The boy [to carry] the books for the teacher.	12	7	14
2	Caveman [to bring] the dinosaur to the back door.	18	3	21
3	He [to hurry] into the classroom.	10	17	22
4	The bird [to fly] over their heads.	4	6	13
5	She [to cross] the street at the corner.	3	9	16
6	Willy [to wash] his hands before breakfast.	8	17	23
7	Elizabeth [to watch] colour TV.	18	6	12
8	The dog always [to wait] for me at the door.	2	6	22
9	Charlie [to do] his homework, too.	16	21	24
10	Kevin [to give] Caveman a piece of chocolate.	10	15	17

Find the correct spelling for the 3rd person singular form of the verb!

		-s	-es	-ies			-s	-es	-ies
11	to worry	16	11	1	18	to drink	16	7	6
12	to stop	5	1	19	19	to hurry	23	5	11
13	to say	20	8	13	20	to work	8	2	20
14	to do	5	24	22	21	to fetch	23	3	6
15	to go	1	15	3	22	to watch	4	23	13
16	to take	19	14	24	23	to give	7	11	14
17	to cry	16	18	12	24	to sell	4	8	9

Tip: Signal words for the simple form of the present tense = never, always, often, every day, every week, every ..., *(regelmäßige Handlung)*; present progressive = now, at this moment, look, listen! *(gerade jetzt)*.
Put in the correct signal word!

#	Sentence	Option 1		Option 2	
1	It's 7:30 and they are going to school **?**.	every week	22	now	14
2	Mrs. Schweizer is eating at the restaurant **?**.	at this moment	16	every Saturday	3
3	Mrs. Schweizer eats at the restaurant **?**.	now	13	every Saturday	17
4	Our cat **?** jumps onto the kitchen table.	at this moment	2	never	13
5	Kevin **?** plays his guitar in the afternoon.	always	6	now	17
6	**?** Kevin is playing his electric guitar.	Never	20	Listen!	15
7	**?** The porters are wearing green uniforms.	Look!	4	Always!	11
8	My doctor **?** wears a white jacket.	at this moment	20	often	2
9	The taxi is waiting for them **?**.	at this moment	18	every morning	3
10	The taxi waits at the train station **?**.	every morning	5	now	6
11	She is helping him take off his coat **?**.	never	19	now	1
12	She **?** helps older people with their coats.	now	16	always	3
13	**?** the silly boys are throwing chalk at the girls.	Now	20	Never	4
14	Dolly fetches chalk for the teacher **?**.	now	17	every morning	22
15	**?** Fat Freddy is eating in class again.	Always!	7	Look!	24
16	The thin boy **?** eats anything.	never	19	now	9
17	Mr. Blackburn is washing his silver Rolls-Royce **?**.	now	10	every week	14
18	He washes it **?**.	at the moment	18	every Saturday afternoon	23
19	What are they doing **?** ?	always	13	now	9
20	What do they **?** do?	always	8	now	3
21	They **?** bring their aunt a tree for Christmas.	now	· 7	always	12
22	Mrs. George is putting her budgie into its cage **?**.	now	21	on Wednesday	11
23	**?** The alarm clock is ringing.	Always!	1	Listen!	7
24	Does the bank **?** close at 3 o'clock?	at this moment	5	always	11

Shopping at the Supermarket

Simple Present or Present Progressive?

1 Mrs. Schweizer always **?** a pound of sugar.
is buying • 16   buys • 23

2 The shop-assistant **?** tins on the shelf now.
is putting • 19   puts • 2

3 Kevin and Andy never **?** away glass bottles.
are throwing • 20   throw • 10

4 Look! Fat Freddy **?** two baskets.
is carrying • 12   carries • 11

5 Now Caveman **?** the cash desk.
picks up • 14   is picking up • 9

6 Mr. Bingham **?** shopping every Saturday.
goes • 8   is going • 22

7 I **?** my money at this moment.
am counting • 7   count • 1

8 Miss Root always **?** a box of eggs before buying them.
is opening • 24   opens • 11

9 **?** you got a loaf of bread?
Have • 21   Having • 15

10 Mum often **?** her change.
is forgetting • 19   forgets • 22

11 Listen! The manager **?** to a customer.
talks • 17   is talking • 24

12 Dogs must **?** outside.
wait • 20   waiting • 3

13 My friends often **?** shopping at the other supermarket.

are going • 8   go • 5

14 Joe **?** at the other supermarket at this moment.

shops • 9   is shopping • 1

15 Every Tuesday they **?** hot bread.

are selling • 6   sell • 3

16 We **?** to go to modern supermarkets.

like • 18   are liking • 19

17 Look! Jennifer **?** cornflakes out of the packet.

eats • 11   is eating • 13

18 Oh no! A hungry dog **?** a bone right now.

is taking • 16   takes • 14

19 We always **?** our things in a basket.

are putting • 4   put • 2

20 Look! A cat **?** in this box here.

is lying • 17   lies • 21

21 Those two women **?** each other every Monday.

see • 15   are seeing • 12

22 The shop-assistant always **?** your bag to the car.

carries • 14   is carrying • 5

23 The supermarket **?** at this moment.

is closing • 6   closes • 2

24 The supermarket **?** every morning at eight o'clock.

is opening • 20   opens • 4

Which question word asks the right question?

How many   sisters have you got? ➜ I have got   two   sisters.

1   Where does the train arrive? • 17
    When does the train arrive? • 3   The train arrives
                                                      at ten o'clock .

2   What arrives in three minutes? • 1
    When does the bus arrive? • 6   The bus arrives
                                                      in three minutes.

3   Who is in the bus? • 13   There are 14 passengers
    How many passengers are in the bus? • 18   in the bus.

4   Who is late? • 16   The passengers
    Why are the passengers late? • 14   are late.

5   Where is Ursula sitting? • 20   Ursula is sitting
    Who is sitting in the last seat? • 23   in the last seat.

6   What is on the floor? • 3   My suitcase is
    Where is my suitcase? • 14   on the floor .

7   What colour is the bus stop sign? • 19   The bus stop sign
    What is green and yellow? • 16   is green and yellow .

8   What is he doing? • 6   He is running
    Why is he running? • 21   because he is late .

9   When does the train stop? • 19   The train stops
    Where does the train stop? • 5   in Oxford .

10 What does the porter carry? • 12   The porter carries
    Who carries your suitcase? • 4   your suitcase .

11 Who is going to the party? • 22   Mrs. Jones is going
    Where is Mrs. Jones going? • 10   to the party by bus.

12 Where is the taxi driver driving to? • 24   The taxi driver
    Who is driving to the train station? • 8   is driving to the station.

13 What has Caveman got? • 15   Caveman has got
    Who has got a big thumb? • 1   a big thumb .

14 | Who is walking to London? • 13 | He is walking
| Where is he walking to? • 20 | to London.

15 | Where are the buses? • 6 | There are two buses
| How many buses are at the bus stop? • 17 | at the bus stop.

16 | What is yellow? • 15 | That school bus
| What colour is that school bus? • 4 | is yellow .

17 | What is the tourist wearing? • 19 | A tourist is wearing
| Who is wearing white shoes? • 7 | white shoes.

18 | When must you have some money? • 5 | I must have some money
| What must you have? • 6 | for the train ticket.

19 | Why must you have more money? • 20 | I must have more money
| Who must have more money? • 3 | because it's expensive .

20 | Who wants the passport? • 24 | The customs officer
| What does the customs officer want? • 9 | wants the passport.

21 | What is sitting in that taxi? • 3 | The gorilla is sitting
| Where is the gorilla sitting? • 11 | in that taxi .

22 | Who looks like a gorilla? • 2 | The taxi driver
| What does the taxi driver look like? • 5 | looks like a gorilla.

23 | What is he? • 21 | He is a gorilla
| Why is he a gorilla? • 22 | because there is a party .

24 | Where is the passenger going to? • 24 | The passenger
| Who is going to the zoo? • 15 | is going to the zoo .

Find the Correct Question!

1 | Who is Bill? • 6 | Bill is playing footba
| Where is Bill playing football? • 3 | in the garden

2 | Who always talks in the classroom? • 17 | Sally and Terry alway:
| Where are Sally and Terry? • 2 | talk in the classroom

3 | What is flying to Africa? • 19 | The jet plane is flying
| Where is the plane flying to? • 14 | to Africa

4 | How many brothers and sisters have you got? • 4 | I have got one
| Who is your sister? • 1 | brother and two sisters

5 | What is it? • 3 | The parrot
| Where is the parrot? • 20 | is in its cage

6 | Who drives a car? • 14 | I drive a car
| Why do you drive a car? • 18 | because they can't

7 | Who never picks flowers in the park? • 2 | They never pick
| What do they never pick? • 24 | flowers in the park.

8 | Where can you pick flowers? • 10 | You can pick flowers
| What can you pick? • 17 | in my garden

9 | Who works at the restaurant? • 13 | Mrs. Pearl works
| Where does Mrs. Pearl work? • 20 | at the restaurant.

10 | What colour is the house? • 3 | The house has got
| How many doors has the house got? • 19 | three doors.

11 | Who wants to be a pilot? • 5 | The young lady wants
| What does the young lady want to be? • 9 | to be a pilot .

12 | Who lives in that house? • 14 | The Walkers live
| Where do the Walkers live? • 23 | in that house .

13 | Who is playing jazz? • 21 | The men are playing
| When are the men playing jazz? • 16 | jazz tonight .

14	Why are you sending a present? • 6	I'm sending my cousin
	Who has got a birthday? • 19	a present
		because it is his birthday .
15	Who says the correct answer? • 2	Linda says it is
	What does she say? • 1	the correct answer.
16	Why are you twelve? • 16	I'm
	How old are you? • 15	twelve years old .
17	What does he want? • 11	He wants a stamp
	Why does he want a stamp? • 7	for his letter.
18	Who likes to walk? • 4	Anthony likes to walk
	Where does Anthony like to walk? • 1	in the mountains .
19	What does your cat do? • 5	Our cat likes to sleep
	Where does your cat like to sleep? • 12	in a basket .
20	Who sleeps in the classroom? • 21	Willy sleeps
	Where does Willy sleep? • 15	in the classroom.

21	What are the boys doing? • 3	The boys are eating
	What are the boys eating? • 7	apples .
22	What is a blackboard? • 14	Our blackboard
	What colour is your blackboard? • 5	is green .
23	Who is Sally? • 18	Sally is putting the bread
	Where is Sally putting the bread? • 22	on the table .
24	When do the lessons begin? • 8	The lessons begin
	What begins at 8 o'clock? • 15	at 8 o'clock .

Do/Does as an Auxiliary Verb in Questions

Tip: Use "does" in the 3rd person singular!

		Do	Does
1	**?** you smoke cigarettes?	21	3
2	**?** a tiger eat chalk?	24	20
3	**?** Mary and Betty like to dance?	23	4
4	**?** I have egg on my face?	22	16
5	**?** you like hamburgers with ketchup?	17	5
6	**?** tourists really look silly?	19	1
7	**?** your chewing-gum have sugar in it?	15	13
8	**?** your sister listen to disco music?	14	15
9	**?** he always want to be first?	18	24
10	**?** Englishmen always drink tea?	18	2
11	**?** the Scots always drink whisky?	16	9
12	**?** a rabbit have long ears?	12	14
13	**?** rabbits climb trees?	9	17
14	**?** we have everything we need?	7	8
15	**?** she ever forget anything?	20	11
16	**?** I ever forget anything?	10	21
17	**?** Manfred ask silly questions?	17	2
18	**?** his dog drink warm milk?	19	12
19	**?** your dog follow you to school?	4	1
20	**?** the bad weather make you sad?	22	3
21	**?** it make you happy?	5	6
22	**?** they get up early?	8	14
23	**?** Ralph like girls?	16	4
24	**?** the bell ring every hour?	9	5

Short Answers

1	Does Tim's father play tennis?	Yes,	he doesn't • 8	he does • 15
2	Can Frank find his pen?	No,	he can • 23	he can't • 17
3	Do you drink tea?	No,	I do • 13	I don't • 14
4	Can an elephant fly?	No,	it can't • 16	it can • 20
5	Does a cat eat fish?	Yes,	it does • 13	it doesn't • 2
6	Does Tina like to dance?	Yes,	she doesn't • 1	she does • 24
7	Do I have a bad cold?	No,	I do • 12	I don't • 5
8	Does Jim have a cold?	Yes,	he does • 3	he doesn't • 22
9	Do we have exercise-books?	Yes,	we don't • 4	we do • 19
10	Do you like to have fun?	Yes,	I don't • 9	I do • 2
11	Does Tom like coffee?	Yes,	he doesn't • 23	he does • 4
12	Does Debbie ride a bike?	No,	she doesn't • 18	she does • 17
13	Do Tony and Sue have bikes?	Yes,	they don't • 6	they do • 21
14	Does Kevin teach Caveman?	Yes,	he does • 23	he doesn't • 4
15	Can a dog drink water?	Yes,	it can't • 15	it can • 7
16	Do you forget things?	Yes,	I do • 22	I don't • 14
17	Can they forget things?	Yes,	they can't • 8	they can • 11
18	Can he play football?	Yes,	he can • 20	he can't • 24
19	Do elephants forget things?	No,	they don't • 6	they do • 17
20	Do disc jockeys play music?	Yes,	they don't • 4	they do • 9
21	Do you have my telephone number?	No,	I do • 10	I don't • 1
22	Does the sun shine?	Yes,	it does • 12	it doesn't • 5
23	Is it 12 o'clock?	No,	it is • 7	it isn't • 10
24	Is this the last question?	Yes,	it is • 8	it isn't • 19

Asking Questions (Word Order)

Question word	Auxiliary Verb	Subject	Verb	Object
Where	can	the man	eat	lunch?
What	has	Tom	got	in his bag?
	Do	you	speak	English?

Man braucht ein Hilfsverb, um eine Frage zu stellen!
Meistens nimmt man eine Form von "do".
Where <u>does</u> she play it? She plays it in her room.

Ausnahme: wenn man nach dem Subjekt des Satzes fragt (kein "do").
Who plays the piano? Martha plays the piano.

Which question is correct? *(Vorsicht: Eine Antwort ist grammatikalisch falsch!)*

1. When plays Tim tennis? | 4 **?** When does Tim play tennis? | 13
2. What can I do for you? | 17 **?** What can I for you do? | 15
3. Speak you German? | 11 **?** Do you speak German? | 4
4. Where live you? | 21 **?** Where do you live? | 2
5. Must Bill his room clean? | 19 **?** Must Bill clean his room? | 3
6. When begins the match? | 18 **?** When does the match begin? | 6
7. Who plays the trumpet? | 5 **?** Who does the trumpet play? | 24
8. How many hamburgers eat you? | 17 **?** How many hamburgers can you eat? |
9. How many bikes have you? | 21 **?** How many bikes do you have? | 15
10. Sell you bananas? | 23 **?** Do you sell bananas? | 16
11. Watch you colour TV? | 5 **?** Do you watch colour TV? | 14
12. Watches Peter colour TV? | 6 **?** Does Peter watch colour TV? | 18
13. Does your cat like to eat fish? | 7 **?** Like your cat fish to eat? | 19
14. Can the stewardess a plane fly? | 12 **?** Can the stewardess fly a plane? | 11
15. Must a mouse eat cheese? | 9 **?** Must a mouse cheese eat? | 3
16. Does your dog fetch the newspaper? | 20 **?** Fetch your dog the newspaper? |
17. Do you understand the question? | 23 **?** Understand you the question? | 8
18. Does Monika it understand? | 8 **?** Does Monika understand it? | 22
19. Who flies a plane? | 12 **?** Who does a plane fly? | 3
20. Where has an answer? | 16 **?** Who has an answer? | 19
21. What colour is the pencil? | 21 **?** What colour the pencil has? | 13
22. What time is it? | 24 **?** Have you the time? | 15
23. Why play you football? | 18 **?** Why do you play football? | 8
24. Like you sardines? | 6 **?** Do you like sardines? | 10